SEASON

JESUS THE
GAME CHANGER
TO THE ENDS OF THE EARTH

DISCUSSION GUIDE

SERIES HOST
KARL FAASE

13 Sessions for Churches and
Discussion Groups.

WRITTEN BY
DR VIVIAN GRICE

To be used in conjunction with
*Jesus the Game Changer Season
Two* documentary series.

WWW.JESUSTHEGAMECHANGER.COM

Authentic

JESUS THE GAME CHANGER SEASON TWO
DISCUSSION GUIDE

First published October 2019
Copyright 2019 Olive Tree Media Limited

Jesus the Game Changer Season Two
Discussion Guide is produced by

Authentic Media Limited
PO Box 6326
Bletchley
Milton Keynes
MK1 9GG
Email:
info@authenticmedia.co.uk
www.authenticmedia.co.uk
under licence from

Olive Tree Media Limited
PO Box 1007 Sutherland
NSW 1499 Australia

Email: info@olivetreemedia.com.au
www.olivetreemedia.com.au
www.jesusthegamechanger.com

ISBN 978-1-78893-140-3

All Scripture quotations are taken from the Holy Bible, New
International Version.

Graphic Design by Mezzanine
Printed and bound by CPI Group (UK) Ltd., Croydon, CR0 4YY

CONTENTS

INTRODUCTION

Christianity is a global religion. It transcends cultures, national boundaries, social classes and geographical divisions. It does not privilege a particular human language. It is not wedded to specific organisational structures. It does not favour one racial group or culture. And this world-wide spread commenced very early on in the church's history. Within mere decades of the resurrection of Jesus in 33AD, His message burst out of the land of its birth, Israel. It raced beyond through the boundaries of the (Roman) empire that had sought to quench it. On the way it challenged and increasingly transformed the moral values of that empire. Then it swept beyond the borders of the Roman imperium into the wider world. Why and how did the followers of Jesus, from the very beginning, willingly take the message of Jesus to the *very ends of the earth*? What drove ordinary women and men, to leave comfort and familiarity, face difficulty and danger, and often encounter death itself, to share Jesus with other human beings different from them? And how does that trajectory continue today in our globalised world? That is the focus of this series. It's a challenging and exciting story.

KARL FAASE & VIVIAN GRICE

DISCUSSION GUIDE

The purpose of this discussion guide is to allow participants who watch *Jesus the Game Changer Season Two* to discuss the content and explore the influence of Jesus in the world. The guide will provide the enquiring, the sceptical and believer alike, the opportunity to explore vital questions which emerge from a consideration of the impact that Jesus has had and why it matters today.

Our aim with this guide is to provide an environment for open, reflective and honest questions emerging from the subjects of each episode.

This guide is designed to help small groups navigate the material in *Jesus the Game Changer Season Two* in a manner that will help stimulate discussion and bring the issues into real life situations. Participants will be given the opportunity to consider how the key ideas presented in the series might impact their lives.

A group leader or facilitator should read this material prior to the group watching the relevant episode together. This should take around 30 minutes.

Once the group has viewed the episode, work through the discussion guide, using the readings and questions to assist and as a stimulus for conversation.

GROUP DISCUSSION

Here are some suggestions on how to approach the discussion:

Don't worry about necessarily trying to complete all the questions. Decide as a group which ones to focus on and allow the discussion to go where it takes you. These are big topics to discuss and there's no need to rush through them all.

Encourage honesty and a genuine wrestling with the issue at hand. Some of the topics may raise some emotions, fears and enthusiasms and these are best dealt with in a safe and open manner.

Expect and allow for very different responses to the topics covered. We all have different experiences to bring to the discussion. Diverse interpretations will enrich the discussion and are to be welcomed. Considerate and respectful listening will aid the process immeasurably.

Try to make a priority of the questions that elicit a practical response and application to real life as experienced by each participant.

Some additional material in the form of video interviews is available from the web (for these links go to the *Jesus the Game Changer* app). Consider having participants watch these together or encourage to view them later.

"I THINK THE POWER OF THE GOSPEL WAS THAT EACH INDIVIDUAL WAS BELOVED OF GOD. AS BOTH PAUL AND PETER WILL SAY IN THE NEW TESTAMENT, GOD SHOWS NO FAVOURITISM. THAT, YOU WOULD NOT HEAR FROM A ROMAN."

LYNN COHICK

EPISODE 1
JESUS OF NAZARETH

INTRODUCTION

In current times, Christianity is not the only global religion. Accelerated in part by modern communication systems and migration, a handful of other faiths have spread around the globe. Christianity, however, claims the largest number of adherents.

So, what is different about Christian faith in its early and current global, transformative reach? A key answer is the one who is the centre of its worship and loyalty, Jesus. From an obscure Jewish village in a small first century AD Roman province, Jesus emerged and over a three year period was hailed as the expected Jewish Messiah. There were others who claimed that title. They all faded out or were executed. Their efforts ended there.

In the end, Jesus too was executed by the Romans in a profoundly brutal, shameful way (crucifixion). It should have ended there. It didn't. Jesus' followers soon began to boldly call all people, not just Jews, to follow Him as Lord of all the world.

Why? The answer was the resurrection of Jesus. Utterly convinced that Jesus had risen from death, His followers testified (and testify still) to the profound change He brought to them. The Christian faith did not spread by armies conquering territory. It spread through the transformation of individuals who then carried the message of Jesus to the ends of the earth. As their God was a missionary God, so Christians became a missionary people.

WATCH EPISODE 1 'JESUS OF NAZARETH'

GETTING STARTED

The Christian faith is founded on the real Jesus of history. Read the following New Testament passages that introduce us to this person:

Luke 1:1-4; 3:21-23; John 1:1-14; Philippians 2:6-11; Colossians 1:15-20; Hebrews 1:1-3.

REFLECTION

What are your earliest memories of hearing about Jesus and what did you hear?

As you read the above passages, what impresses you about what is recorded concerning Jesus?

DISCUSSION

1   Discuss the relative importance of the following components for an authentic Christian life:

       (i)   a set of moral values

       (ii) the nature, person and work of Jesus

       (iii a community/church experience

       (iv) a religious experience

2 What would it matter for the Christian faith if it was proved that Jesus' resurrection was not true?

3 The participants in the episode point to at least four key things that made and make Jesus such a transformative figure worldwide:

- His teaching on the value and equality of all people - *"each individual was beloved of God."* [Lynn Cohick]

- the death of Jesus on the cross – *"this symbol of death ultimately becomes a symbol of new life."* [Ed Stetzer]

- the resurrection of Jesus – *"the cornerstone of our faith … Jesus is alive, He is also Lord of the universe."* [Craig Keener]

- Jesus' continuing impact on people today – *"He changed my life and that's the way I see Jesus as the Game Changer."* [Maryam Rostampour]

Why are these so important? Which is most or least persuasive for you?

4   Read 1 Corinthians 15:12-19. What does this passage have to say about the implications of the resurrection for Christian faith?

5   Read Psalm 67 and John 3:16-21. In the episode, Ermias Mamo makes this observation: *"When we see the whole Scripture, we realise God is a missionary God. And the Bible is a missionary book. The things He taught, the task He has given to the Church. Go and preach the Gospel. Make disciples."* What motivations do you discover from the passages and the episode that encourage you to take up the mission of Jesus?

6   How do you respond to Maryam and Marziyeh's story of coming to faith in Jesus, being changed by Him, and deciding to share that with their friends and family in spite of the danger?

ACTION

In the coming week, make time to read through or listen to the whole of Mark's Gospel, in one sitting if possible.

Spend some time this week developing a two sentence, memorable ending to one of the following statements:

"I am a follower of Jesus because ..."

OR

"I am interested in knowing more about Jesus because ..."

OR

"I am curious about the person of Jesus because ..."

"BY ABOUT 70AD THE CHURCH SPREAD IN PARTS OF THE TRANS-JORDAN, JUST ACROSS THE JORDAN RIVER. IT'S IN SYRIA, IT'S IN EGYPT, IT'S PROBABLY IN NORTH AFRICA. SO, THERE WAS THIS VERY VIBRANT CHURCH ACROSS THE STEPS OF ASIA, PERSIA... ALL THE WAY THROUGH TO INDIA AND CHINA. YOU DON'T HEAR A LOT ABOUT IT BUT THERE'S ACTUALLY QUITE A SIGNIFICANT HISTORY OF THE CHURCH OUT THERE."

MICHAEL BIRD

EPISODE 2
PAUL & THE EARLY CHURCH

INTRODUCTION

Within seventy years of Jesus' death and resurrection, the movement that began with Him had spread with great rapidity. Along trade routes it surged south into what is present day Ethiopia, east into present day Iraq and Iran, and its tide washed possibly as far as India. Likewise, it ran swiftly westward to Spain and modern France.

A key player in these early days was a Jew named Saul, later renamed Paul. Originally a violent persecutor of Jesus' followers, Saul underwent an abrupt, dramatic, 180 degree conversion. This experience turned him from a fanatical persecutor of Jesus into a courageous and passionate promoter of His message. And with that message he led a movement that spread out across the globe. Travelling back and forth across the Mediterranean, planting small groups of new Christians, writing letters to those churches, setting an example of mission work, Paul established the pattern for following generations of believers to take the message of Jesus to the ends of the earth.

WATCH EPISODE 2 'PAUL & THE EARLY CHURCH'

GETTING STARTED

Read the three accounts of Paul's dramatic conversion found in Acts 9:1-19, 22:1-21 and 26:9-23.

REFLECTION

Jesus taught and practised that all people mattered equally to God. Paul announced, *"the idea that Christ died for all of humanity."* The accompanying truth was that *"there is no Jew or Greek"* (Galatians 5:26-29), *".... that difference is dissolved ..."* [Tom Holland]. In what ways were these ideas revolutionary, when they emerged? How much do they still matter today to (a) followers of Jesus, (b) Western culture and (c) the wider world?

Have you ever encountered the kind of 'Damascus road' experience that Saul (Paul) underwent? Do you accept it, question it, doubt it or embrace it?

DISCUSSION

1   Karl lists four factors that he sees as important for the swift spread of Christian faith to the ends of the earth;

      (i)   the validity of Jesus' life;

      (ii) the evidence for Him being the Son of God, not just another religious teacher;

(iii) Jesus 'sending' His followers into the world; and

(iv) the power of the Spirit in people's lives.

What do you think about this argument?

2 Dana Robert considers the concept of a *"network"* or *"chain"* in the life of each of Jesus' followers, linking them, ultimately, back to Jesus, His people the Jews and His call from God.

In your group, share the various chain links that have brought you to this point in your faith journey.

3 A key link in the chain that formed the spread of early Christianity was the radical conversion of Saul from fanatical persecutor of Christians to passionate promoter of their faith. Read the story of that conversion in Acts 9:1-19a.

How do you react to this account?

4   Read Romans 15:23-33. What strikes you about this personal expression of Paul's life work?

5   Tom Holland indicates that Paul's decisive teaching was that *"Christ died for all of humanity. So not just for the Jews. … there is no Jew or Greek … that difference is dissolved, that Christ has come for the whole of humanity …"*

Why was this such a transformative concept? Why might it be of great relevance to our world today?

6   In the episode, Mark Noll makes this comment: *"Early Christianity spread, yes because the message was effective, yes because the person of Jesus was attractive but perhaps mostly because Christians were simply there, … to do acts of kindness, humanity, outreach in situations where Roman culture did not smile favourably on that kind of person-to-person, group-to-group outreach."*

After reading 1 Peter 3:13-17, discuss Mark's observation linking message and action in the early spread of the Church.

7 How was the favouring of Christianity under the Emperor Constantine a good thing or a bad thing for the spread of the faith?

8 How do you react to Hassan John's narrative in the episode? How would you apply the lessons in your cultural setting, especially if there is no overt physical danger or persecution?

ACTION

Spend some time this week identifying and making notes about key features of the cultural groups (e.g. work, neighbourhood, sporting group, hobby group) among which you live beyond 'church-world'.

Identify some intentional *"acts of kindness, humanity, outreach"* that you can practice in those groups. Choose one and do it. Pray for the opportunity to share the message of Jesus alongside the action taken.

"OUR CONCERN FOR THE WEST IS WE SEE A DIFFERENT LEVEL OF PERSECUTION COMING. AND WE BEGIN TO WONDER IF THE WEST CAN STAND...I WOULD SAY OUR PLEA FOR THE CHURCH IN THE WEST IS NEVER GIVE UP THIS FAITH THAT WE ARE DYING FOR IN AFRICA"

HASSAN JOHN

EPISODE 3

THE PERSECUTED CHURCH

INTRODUCTION

Persecution is defined as "harassment, oppression or maltreatment" because of race, religion or belief. It runs like a scarlet thread through all the history of the Church. From their earliest days, followers of Jesus have faced varying degrees of oppression, opposition, and violence at different periods. In the end, this is because of their ultimate allegiance to Jesus. He predicted that this would be the case (John 15:18-20). Acts 5, 6 & 7 recorded that it swiftly became a reality.

The causes of persecution vary. Other religions oppose the expansion of Christianity, or even the presence of Christian people. Totalitarian governments wanting ultimate allegiance from their citizens seek to crush Christians whose final loyalties are with Jesus. Alternative worldviews fight against Christian values that confront them. Power-hungry groups threaten Christians who seek to support justice or freedom for all. Levels of persecution also vary; from outright, sometimes mortal, violence, through legislated restrictions, to mockery or ridicule.

Whatever the cause or level of persecution, it will occur as followers of Jesus seek to share His message to the ends of the earth. And often, we will discover that persecution can lead to growth in the life of the Church.

WATCH EPISODE 3 'THE PERSECUTED CHURCH'

GETTING STARTED

Read John 15:18-16:4; Acts 5:17-42; 6:8-7:5.

REFLECTION

Think about this statement by Karl, at the commencement of the episode: *"In the 20th Century, potentially more people lost their lives than any time before that for the message of Jesus. It tells us that when people have taken the message of Jesus to the ends of the earth, people have paid for it with their lives."*

What feelings and thoughts do you have when you read this?

DISCUSSION

1   As Brian Stanley observes, for Christians, persecution can be an outcome of their ultimate allegiance to Jesus. Why is this the case and can you think of Biblical examples?

2   Read the story of Peter and John in Acts 4:1-20. What does this incident say to us and our churches today?

3 One command of God is to share Jesus with others. In some countries this is forbidden. What other commands of Scripture might invite persecution and oppression, whether by governments, family or other people?

4 Christians in the West today, often decry the rise of secularism. Why is living in a secular state a benefit when it comes to potential persecution for being a Christian?

5 How do you respond to the stories of Nii Amoo Darku, Maryam Rostampour, Marziyeh Amirizadeh and Hassan John about the experience of Christians in some Muslim countries?

6 Talk about this comment by Mike Gore: *"But when I look at my own life I feel that the relative safety of culture and the stability of the economic climate that I've grown up in, when I look back it makes* *it more and more difficult to see where the hand of Jesus has been, the highs and the lows. Whereas in the Persecuted Church, they can speak to you for days, for hours, about what Jesus is to them, what He's done in their life, the transformation He brings, why He matters to you."*

7 The Chinese pastor makes this comment to Mike Gore: *"Well, we look at the Australian Church as a prophetic example of what happens when faith becomes free … the value of Jesus drops. I want you to pray persecution never leaves China."*

How do you react to that observation?

8 What, in your opinion, are the main threats to authentic Christian faith in the West?

9 Marziyeh makes this significant comment: *"We can't enjoy just our freedom and forget about those who are still in prison."*

How does this inform your response to the fact that Christians are persecuted all around the world for their (and our) faith?

ACTION

Visit the Open Doors, World Watch site:

https://www.opendoors.org.au/persecuted-christians/world-watch-list/

Find out the top 10 countries in the world where it is most dangerous to be a Christian. Choose one and find out as much as you can about that country. Begin praying for it and believers there. Explore the site and consider how you can further support the Persecuted Church.

"TO BE A MISSIONARY AT THE END OF THE 18TH, EARLY 19TH CENTURY WAS TO BE AN ABOLITIONIST. AND A LOT OF THE DESIRE TO TAKE THE CHRISTIAN GOSPEL TO AFRICA WAS ABOUT REPAIRING A GREAT WRONG, AND WE SEE THIS TIME AND TIME AGAIN. THOSE PEOPLE WHO WERE MISSIONARIES WERE ALSO SUPPORTING THE MOVE TO END SLAVERY."

EMMA WILDWOOD

EPISODE 4
AFRICA

INTRODUCTION

By 2050, half the world's population growth is projected to occur in Africa. It is a huge continent. It covers 30.37 million square kilometres of the earth's surface. There are 54 different nations. It is home to over 1.216 billion people. In 1900AD the number of African Christians was estimated at around 9 million. By 2000AD that number had increased to 380 million. It continues to grow. Some estimates are that there will be 633 million Christian believers by 2025.

The presence of Christian believers on the African continent stretches right back to within mere decades of Jesus' life. Ethiopia was likely the first region to have a native Jesus-follower (Acts 8:26-39). Other early disciples were probably from African soil also (Acts 13:1) – Lucius of Cyrene (a Greek colony in modern day Libya) and Simeon (called Niger, a reference to dark skin colour). For 400 years from around 200AD, Christianity was the dominant religion across north Africa until the Muslim invasions of the late 7th and early 8th centuries. In later centuries, Christian faith followed European traders south around the bulge of West Africa, planting itself on African soil in new locations.

The biggest explosion, in number of Christian believers, has happened in the last 250 years. Missionaries from the northern half of the globe risked health, left family and gave their lives to share the Good News of Jesus with the African south. As Western colonialism ended, the Church expanded swiftly. Now, African Christians are beginning to take the Gospel to the ends of the earth in post-Christian Europe and beyond.

WATCH EPISODE 4 'AFRICA'

GETTING STARTED

In the 19th century Africa was labelled as the 'dark continent' by Europeans. Its interior was still extensively unknown. Its inhabitants were dark skinned. When you think of Africa today, what are the characteristics that you most commonly attribute to it?

REFLECTION

Read and reflect upon Matthew 28:16-20 and Acts 1:7-8.

How would you respond to a call to work in a place where, if you were a foreign worker, the mortality rate was roughly 70% in the first five years?

DISCUSSION

1   Read the account of the conversion of the African traveller in Acts 8:26-39. Why do you think this story is included in the text of Scripture? What do you take from it about Christian mission?

2   What is one fact, from this episode, that has struck you in regard to Christian faith in Africa?

3   What about David Livingstone's life and work is...

- impressive?

- challenging?

- confronting?

- disappointing?

4   Jay Milbrandt noted that David Livingstone, at the end of his life, probably saw himself as a failure. Why was that the case? In what way was he "successful?" How are we to measure success in efforts to take the Gospel to the ends of the earth?

5 Jessie Fubara-Manuel says: *"Mary (Slessor) herself had times when she doubted her call. But … she didn't give up."* Why did Mary (and many other missionaries) not give up?

6 How does Israel Olofinjana's phrase, *"Africans reaching out to Africans"*, as exampled in the story of Samuel Ajayi Crowther, point us to important mission principles?

7 Why, do you think, did African Christianity really start growing strongly after the end of Western colonialism and the beginning of political independence for African nations?

8 What does James McKeown's story tell us about the "power of one," under God's leadership and with a passion for Jesus?

9 Read Revelation 3:14-22. In light of what this episode reveals about Africa, how might this passage be pertinent to the Western Church?

ACTION

Consider this comment by Opoku Onyinah: *"We people in Africa think that the Church in the West now is really suffering. And we keep on praying that God will raise apostles, prophets and evangelists who will be able to break through and revive the Church."* How do you feel about and respond to the sentiments expressed by Opoku?

Go to http://www.globalreligiousfutures.org/countries. Select an African country and research the Christian presence in that nation.

"ONE OF THE MOST UNEXPECTED THINGS THAT HAPPENS IN THE WAKE OF THE FALL OF THE ROMAN EMPIRE IS THAT AN ISLAND THAT HAD NEVER BEEN CONQUERED BY THE ROMANS BECOMES CHRISTIAN. SO, WHILE THE PROVINCE OF BRITANNIA IS BEING RULED BY PAGAN ANGLO-SAXON KINGS, IN IRELAND THE ROOTS OF CHRISTIANITY ARE REACHING DOWN AND BEARING REMARKABLE FRUIT."

TOM HOLLAND

EPISODE 5
IRELAND

INTRODUCTION

Today, Ireland is a popular tourist destination but back in the 5th century AD, Ireland was viewed as "the land of the setting sun" by those who lived in Britain, as it was abandoned by the Roman Empire. Romans thought that there was nothing beyond it. It was a "patchwork of rival kingships" and its people followed a pagan, druidic religion. It was wild and untamed.

Early in the 5th century, a teenage boy named Patrick arrived in this frontier land. The son of a Christian in Britain, he was the victim of human trafficking. Enslaved for around six years he finally escaped back to England. In spite of his harsh experiences, he returned to his home country a transformed young man, with a deep, committed faith in Jesus. In the end, nearly twenty years later, this commitment led him to return to the land of his slave-traders. This time he came as a missionary, determined to carry the message of Jesus to the ends of the earth in Ireland.

So began a remarkable 400 year period in the history of Christianity in Europe. It is a story that in many ways is the account of how Ireland 'saved' Europe as the Roman Empire crumbled in the West. It is the story of a transformed life that led to a transformed culture.

WATCH EPISODE 5 'IRELAND'

GETTING STARTED

Imagine yourself as a teenager, wrenched from home and enslaved in a rough, inhospitable place far away. What would be the likely outcomes for you in terms of your attitude to life and to those around you?

REFLECTION

Read the story of Joseph in Genesis 37:1-36.

What parallels do you see with Patrick's story? What lessons might be learnt from both?

DISCUSSION

1   What surprises you about the story of St Patrick? What most impresses you about his story?

2   Consider the story of Onesimus, a converted slave, in Philemon 1:4-21. What transformations, for Onesimus, Paul and for Philemon occurred because of his conversion to Jesus?

3   Patrick wrote about going *"to the ends of the earth, to the place beyond which no one lives ..."* [Marcus Losack], with the news about Jesus. How might we think about that today?

4   Discuss these words by Joe Turner at the end of the episode: *"... I came to know the King of Kings and the Lord of Lords who came ... and who would have come just for me. That made me a somebody."*

5   What were the changes that happened in Joe's life because he came to faith in Jesus? If you are a follower of Jesus what changes has He made in you? If you are not a follower of Jesus, but there would be some changes you would like to see within yourself, what would they be?

6 Read 2 Corinthians 5:16-21. What are the key ideas in this passage?

7 Why is the message from God, "I love you" so powerful?

8 Read John 1:14. What does the grace of God mean to you?

ACTION

Find some time alone this week to think and pray about what you would truly want for your friends and your community.

NOTES

"THE MISSIONARY STRATEGY WAS TO PLANT COMMUNITIES OF DEDICATED PEOPLE; MONASTERIES, OCCASIONALLY NUNNERIES/CONVENTS FOR WOMEN RELIGIOUS, AND TO SHOW A LOCAL COMMUNITY BY TEACHING INTEGRITY OF LIFE AND EXAMPLE OF LIVING, WHAT THE CHRISTIAN FAITH SHOULD MEAN. SO, AT THEIR BEST, THE MONASTERIES WERE NOT JUST DECLARATIONS OF THE CHRISTIAN FAITH BUT EXEMPLIFICATIONS OF THE CHRISTIAN FAITH."

MARK NOLL

EPISODE 6
EUROPE

INTRODUCTION

In this episode, Karl confesses that his thinking about early medieval monks and monasticism has been radically readjusted. Rather than seeing them as wanting to withdraw and isolate, we discover that they were instrumental in taking the Gospel to England and Europe in the 6th-10th centuries AD. This is especially the case with Irish monasticism, beginning with Patrick. The establishment of this 'Celtic' expression of Christianity proved to be a fertile ground for a line of Irish missionary monks – St. Patrick, St. Aidan, St. Columbus, St. Columbanus, St. Boniface.

These monks bravely carried the Christian message to what was then 'pagan' Europe – Scotland, England, France, Germany, Scandinavia. They did so in the face of great physical danger, both natural and human-made. Whether facing Viking attacks on their monasteries, or confronting pagan religious powers, they gave birth to vibrant, transformational, reproducing Christian communities across the western European continent.

Their missionary strategy? It was simple yet powerful: *"to plant communities of dedicated people, monasteries, ... to show a local community by teaching, integrity of life and example of living what the Christian faith should mean. So, at their best, the monasteries were not just declarations of the Christian faith but exemplifications of the Christian faith."* [Mark Noll]

There are, doubtless, lessons we can learn from these monks as we too face the challenge of taking the message of Jesus to the ends of the earth, especially in a re-paganised Western culture.

WATCH EPISODE 6 'EUROPE'

GETTING STARTED

When you think of monks, what characteristics have typically come to your mind?

Have there been aspects of the stories in this episode that have surprised you?

REFLECTION

Read Ephesians 2:1-13; 1 Peter 1:13-2:3.

The letters of Paul and Peter in the New Testament were written to people whose way of life had been turned around by Jesus Christ whom they followed as Lord. Think about how the truths in these verses were exemplified in some of the stories from this episode.

Do you think, that, like the Christianised Roman Empire, we in the West can tend to believe that Christianity is coterminous (linked) with the West, and so tend to ignore what is happening in the rest of the world?

DISCUSSION

1   How do you respond to the narrative of this episode, that in many ways, Celtic [Irish] Christianity 'saved' Europe for the Christian faith?

2 Mark Noll indicates that the Irish monks did some *"pretty wild things"* in their missionary work. Our society, and often the Church, is much more risk averse. What are the implications for the ongoing call to take the Gospel to the ends of the earth in our day?

3 Eddie Arthur, in this episode, describes the Celtic monks as *"pilgrims for Jesus"*. What do you think he means by this, and how well does it resonate, or not, with how you see yourself in our culture, if you are a follower of Jesus?

4 Why is the story of the Vikings illustrative of the overall narrative of the spread of Christianity to the ends of the earth?

5 Mark Noll says that Boniface was *"an effective confrontational voice for Christian faith."* Ed Stetzer confirms that he *"wasn't this quiet figure."* How do you think that Christians today should balance confrontational and non-confrontational approaches to declaring the message of Jesus to our culture?

6 Irish Christianity was rural and decentralised, whereas the Roman Empire was urbanised and central. How applicable is this to our current culture?

7 The monks' missionary strategy was to plant Christian communities as examples of how to live the Christian life and why it was better. As you think about our era, what strategies do you think should be adopted?

ACTION

Celtic Christian monasticism had important components of prayerful withdrawal and isolation in natural settings, along with commitment to community, learning and mission. In the coming weeks, try setting aside one or more times for a significant period of prayer and reflection (say at least half an hour) in a quiet, natural setting. Leave your phone off for that period. At the end of this time, note any matters about God, self, others that come to mind.

NOTES

"THE IDEAL JESUIT IS LIVING WITH 'ONE FOOT RAISED.' THE SPIRIT THAT WE ALL WANT TO BRING TO WHAT WE'RE DOING, WHETHER RAISING A FAMILY OR WORKING IN A COMPANY OR WORKING IN A CHURCH IS, CAN I HAVE ONE FOOT RAISED? MEANING READY TO GO WHERE THE OPPORTUNITY IS NOW."

CHRIS LOWNEY

EPISODE 7
THE JESUITS

INTRODUCTION

The 16th century was a time of enormous religious tumult in Europe.
Two mighty forces strove for domination: the Protestant Reformation
and the Catholic Counter Reformation. Out of the latter emerged a
converted, brave, aristocratic soldier-turned-missionary, Ignatius
of Loyola. His passionate, disciplined and intelligent faith birthed a
movement that took the Gospel beyond the protective boundaries of
Christian Europe. Inspiring a small band of committed followers, an
organisation emerged that came to be known as the Jesuits. Ignatius
forged a pattern of engaged Christian spirituality, mission and service
that took people such as Matteo Ricci and Francis Xavier to places
as far flung as India, China and Japan. They went to plant the Gospel.
This was well before Protestant missionaries ventured that far.

Embracing the Ignatian precept that Christianity needed to be
immersed in the world rather than sequestered in monastic cloisters,
the Jesuits portrayed qualities that can shape effective leadership
in our own world: self-awareness, ingenuity, heroism and love. This
approach took them to the ends of the earth, into the complexities of
culture and down to the depths of sacrifice for Jesus.

WATCH EPISODE 7 'THE JESUITS'.

GETTING STARTED

Read Matthew 13:44-46. Why, in your opinion, did Jesus tell the parable found there?

REFLECTION

Would you describe yourself as an "heroic" person? Do you think that you are really here for a purpose greater than yourself?

DISCUSSION

1   Ignatius appears to have often been impetuous, driven by enthusiasm out of his new-found passion for Christ. Discuss the relative importance of fervent passion, adventurous enthusiasm, wise caution, astute planning and bold risk-taking in:

- the life of following Jesus
- your life
- the work of the Church
- taking the Gospel to others

2   Dana Robert, Chris Lowney and Tim Kesicki all make the important point that Ignatius gathered around him a group, a band of brothers eventually forming the Jesuits, as he began his task of mission to the ends of the earth. Why was and is such a community an important step for discipleship and the work of mission? Reflect on this in the light of Luke 6:12-15.

3   Chris Lowney refers to four aspects about effective leadership that he believes can be learnt from the Jesuits:

    i.   self-awareness
    ii. ingenuity
    iii. heroism
    iv. love

Discuss these four qualities in light of Jesus' words about 'greatness' in Matthew 20:20-28.

4   How do you respond to Chris Lowney's definition of heroism: *"that fundamentally you'd live in such a way that you cared about something bigger than yourself"*?

5 Mark Noll observes that the Jesuits were boldly prepared to go out beyond the protection of European Christian political power in taking the Gospel to the ends of the earth. How much do you think that the risk-aversion society in which we live has infected followers of Jesus, and hindered the spread of the Gospel today?

6 Dana Robert suggests that the *"intense spirituality"* of the Jesuits enabled them to survive in any worldly setting. Read Romans 12:1-2. What kind of spiritual practices do we need to survive as Jesus' people in our current setting so that we are less likely to be squeezed into the world's mould?

7 Read John 15:18-20, 16:31-33; 1 John 2:15-17. What do you think about Tim Kesicki's assertion about the Jesuits, that *"'the world is good' ... Ignatius said 'no, go live in the world, and that everything in the world can be used for good.' ... So, he loved the world."*

ACTION

Keep an inventory of your actual spiritual practices this week.

Think about one heroic thing that you could do for Christ, within your own current world. Attempt to put it into practise this week.

"TO REALISE THE COST THAT THEY PAID TO BE OBEDIENT AND TO BE FAITHFUL TO GOD'S CALL IN THEIR LIFE, IS A SIGNIFICANT REMINDER TO EACH SUBSEQUENT GENERATION THAT TO BE FAITHFUL IS NOT NECESSARILY AN EASY ROAD. AND IN FACT, MORE OFTEN THAN NOT, IT'S A ROAD THAT COMES WITH TESTING, COMES WITH DIFFICULTIES. AND HOW CAN I BE FAITHFUL IN MY GENERATION?"

JAMIE TAYLOR

EPISODE 8
CHINA

INTRODUCTION

China, today, is the world's most populous nation. It is also, according to Open Doors, the twenty-seventh most difficult place in the world to be a Christian. Yet the number of Jesus' followers there is growing steadily. It may, sometime within the 21st century, host the largest Christian community on the planet.

Surprisingly, Christians have existed in China since the mid-600s AD. This far eastern nation has been repeatedly visited by a diversity of courageous, missionary-minded believers. First, there were traders along the Silk Road in the 7th century. Then Jesuit missionaries arrived in the 1600s. Finally, the biggest wave came through Protestant evangelicals in the 19th and 20th centuries. For over 1400 hundred years, Jesus' followers have sought to take His Good News to this enormous, far-flung area.

Persecution has surged periodically throughout the Church's life in China. One such era arose when Communists took control in 1949. The country became much more closed to the outside world. Missionaries were forced to leave. Departing, they feared that the Church would quickly succumb to the pressure. However, when greater openness returned in the 1970s, a vibrant, bold, growing Christian community had flourished. This growth has continued until today, despite recent renewed pressure from the Communist regime. And this Church, having received its Christianity from the West, is now continuing the Church's mission back towards the West. Today, Chinese Christians are heeding the call of Jesus to take His Word to the ends of the earth.

WATCH EPISODE 8 'CHINA'

GETTING STARTED

Is there anything that surprises you about the history of a Christian presence in China? If so, what?

REFLECTION

Consider the advantages, obstacles and challenges that faced missionaries heading into China up to the 20th century. Compare those challenges with the advantages, challenges and obstacles that we might face today in going to China to share the Good News of Jesus.

DISCUSSION

1   Consider the following passages: 1 Chronicles 16:22-24; Psalm 66:1-4; Isaiah 45:20-25. China was not known at all to these Old Testament writers. What might these passages have to say about God's view of the world's people?

2 Daryl Ireland notes that when Christianity first came to China, it was known as the *"luminous religion"*. Why do you think it was given this name and how do you respond to that title? What name do you think might be given to Christianity in your country today?

3 Matteo Ricci dressed as a Chinese when he went into China as a missionary. Why? How was this an implementation of the verses in 1 Corinthians 9:19-23? How might the practices outlined by Paul be applied in your setting today?

4 Daryl Ireland explains how Hudson Taylor, in going to China, adopted a mission principle of *"the Gospel is going to you"* rather than *"you come to us"*. How might you and your church pursue such a practice today?

5 What is inspiring about the Cambridge Seven?

6 How do you personally respond to CT Studd's comment that *"Some people want to live within the sound of a church or a chapel bell. I want to set up a rescue shop within one yard of Hell"*?

7 Read Matthew 16:21-28; Luke 8:19-21. Why are these verses pertinent to people such as Hudson Taylor and Os Guinness's family's obedience to God in going to 19th century China with the Gospel?

ACTION

Costly obedience and persecution have been marks of the Church in China from earliest missionary days. Take some time this week to:

    (i)   reflect on the cost of your obedience to Christ

    (ii) what persecution (or discrimination) you have experienced for your faith in Christ, if you follow Him.

NOTES

"LUTHER GRASPED THAT PAUL WAS TALKING ABOUT A RIGHTEOUSNESS THAT GOD GIVES FREELY. ANY RIGHTEOUSNESS THAT WE EXPERIENCE IS NOT OUR WORK BUT GOD'S WORK IN US. THIS WAS REVOLUTIONARY. THIS WAS GRACE. THIS WAS GOD'S UNMERITED FAVOUR. LUTHER WOULD LATER WRITE, 'WHEN I DISCOVERED THIS, I WAS BORN AGAIN OF THE HOLY GHOST AND THE DOORS OF PARADISE SWUNG OPEN, AND I WALKED THROUGH.'"

KARL FAASE

THE PROTESTANT REFORMATION

INTRODUCTION

Many of us have heard of Luther's 95 Theses, posted on the door of a church in Wittenberg, Germany. They were a list of discussion points, written in Latin, for an academic debate by theologians. Yet this list of points for debate ended up igniting a religious revolution in 16th century Christian Europe. It became known as "The Protestant Reformation." This revolution then swept gradually around the globe.

The movement was made possible by at least four factors:

i. the brilliance and courage of a German scholar-monk named Martin Luther

ii. a set of theological ideas about how people are put right with God, which struck a deep chord with common people

iii. a political leader who provided protection for Luther, the religious "radical"

iv. the technology of mass printing that enabled Luther's ideas to spread with tremendous rapidity in everyday language.

The Protestant Reformation of the Church was so-called because Luther "protested" against certain aspects of medieval Church practices. This protest by a single monk eventually spawned vibrant new Christian movements and denominations, which further helped to take the Gospel to the ends of the earth.

WATCH EPISODE 9 'THE PROTESTANT REFORMATION'

GETTING STARTED

Read Romans 1:8-17 in three different translations.

REFLECTION

What are four major points Paul is making in Romans 1:8-17?

DISCUSSION

1   Share and discuss your answers to the *"Reflection"* question.

2 Eric Metaxas described Martin Luther as *"a larger than life figure who was such a maniac, such a crazy, funny, entertaining figure."* What do you think about the suggestions that the Church in the West today needs some kind of revolution? If so, what would such a revolution consist of, and do we need more *"crazy, funny, entertaining"* leaders in the Church today?

3 The printing press was the means of distributing Luther's ideas extremely widely and rapidly. What are the advantages and disadvantages of modern modes of communication for the Church's effort to take the Gospel to a wide audience?

4 Karl makes the point that Luther's posting of the 95 Theses was also driven by a fresh understanding of how God puts people right with Himself, based on Romans 1:17. What is meant by this verse? What does it tell us about the Christian view of grace?

5 When asked by the religious authorities to recant his views, Luther stood his ground thoughtfully, and refused. He was prepared to die for what he had come to believe. What are the things that you would be prepared to die for, as far as you can say now?

6 One of the side effects of Luther's revolution, was that he translated the Bible into the language of the common people. These Bibles were then rapidly reproduced by the printing press. Consequently, the common people could own a copy. Dana Robert makes this observation: *"Over time the Bible in the home becomes a core part of Protestant spirituality."* What are the indications in your life about whether or not the Bible is a core part of your spirituality?

7 Why was Luther's marriage to Katharina von Bora, a former nun, a significant, symbolic step in Luther's challenge to the existing Church practices?

8 Luther began to wonder whether, behind the forces arrayed against him, the Devil was really at work. How do you decide whether the Devil is at work in certain circumstances or not?

9 What are some of the implications of putting God utterly first in life, as did Luther [Eric Metaxas]?

ACTION

Write a one sentence response to someone who asked you this question: *"How can I get right with God?"*

Make a list of your core beliefs, about which you could say, as did Luther in the face of immense pressure to recant, *"So here I stand, I can do no other, so help me God."*

"THE BEAUTY AND THE GLORY OF CHRISTIANITY IS THAT WE BELIEVE GOD WORKS IN ALL DIFFERENT LANGUAGES. THE ACT OF BIBLE TRANSLATION IS THE ACT OF GIVING PEOPLE GOD'S WORD IN THEIR OWN LANGUAGE. IT'S REALLY THE HEART OF WHAT PROTESTANT MISSION HAS BEEN SINCE THE TIME OF MARTIN LUTHER."

DANA ROBERT

EPISODE 10
BIBLE TRANSLATION

INTRODUCTION

From the very beginning of the Church, Jesus' followers have been people whose faith was expressed in written form. They read the Old Testament as telling God's story which led up to Jesus. Then they wrote about their experiences of God in Christ, putting them down in letters, Gospels and histories. These documents were discerned by the Church, in a relatively short space of time, as being inspired by God. Eventually, they were collected into what we now know as the Bible.

This collection of books was originally written in three languages: Hebrew, Aramaic and Greek. However, in their desire to communicate the message of Jesus to the ends of the earth, Christians began to translate the Bible into the languages of the people with whom they shared that message. This pattern repeated itself across the history of the Church. Today the Bible, or part of it, has been translated into around 2900 languages.

The importance of this has been that over the last two thousand years, and across multiple cultures, people from around the globe have been able to hear and respond to the message of Jesus in their heart language. Bible translation is a key means of communicating the message of Jesus. That has been particularly the case with Protestant mission efforts. It is a task people have given their lives to, and sometimes their lives for. And that task continues today.

WATCH EPISODE 10 'BIBLE TRANSLATION'

GETTING STARTED

How do you respond to this statement by Robert Woodberry:

> *"Where you had greater Protestant missionary influence, you have higher literacy, higher school enrolment, more newspaper circulation, more book circulation, more voluntary association membership, higher GDP, more medical hospital beds, longer life expectancy, lower infant mortality, lower corruption, and greater political democracy."*

REFLECTION

Imagine not being able to read or being able to read but not having a Bible in your language. What impact do you think that would have on your life as a follower and worshipper of Jesus, or if you were someone wanting to know more about Jesus?

DISCUSSION

1   Dana Robert makes this comment: *"Bible translation makes the point that God does not have only one language."* What do you think is meant by this, and why is it important?

2 Read Exodus 34:1-4; 2 Kings 22:1-13; Luke 1:1-4; Romans 10:9-15; Colossians 4:10-16; Revelation 2. Why might these passages be important for the issues of Bible translation, faith, mission and the written word of God?

3 Tefera Endalew makes this comment: *"You and me, we are the result of translation work."* In what ways does this apply to Christians? In what way does it apply to any society shaped by the Christian faith?

4 What is the link between the Bible, missionary work, printing and literacy?

5 We might be tempted to think that translation work is quite a desk-bound and safe job. Why is that not the case when it comes to translating languages for the first time?

6 As you listen to the stories of the Wycliffe missionaries, Tefera, Eddie, Kirk, and Takashi, what principles for communicating the Gospel to others, can you discern, that might apply to your situation, even if you are dealing with people whose language and culture you share?

7 Why was it the case in the early days of Wycliffe Bible Translators that so many single women played crucial roles in that work?

8 Read Romans 10:9-15 again. How does Paul link faith, mission and the written word of God?

ACTION

Do some research on these questions:

(a) What is the world's human population at present?

(b) How many languages still do not have

(i) a complete Bible

(ii) or a part of the Bible translated?

(c) How many people have NO portion of the Bible in their language?

(d) How many people do not have a FULL Bible in their language?

What is your response to these statistics?

"THE KOREAN CHURCH IS SPIRITUALLY INDEBTED. WE HAVE TO PAY BACK THE DEBT. THERE IS NOTHING ELSE WE HAVE TO DO. THE MISSION FOR THE KOREAN CHURCH IS TO REACH OUT TO PEOPLE WHO HAVE NOT HEARD AND ARE WAITING FOR THE GOSPEL TO COME AND SERVE THEM WITH OUR WHOLE HEART."

SUNG-YOUNG KIM

EPISODE 11
JAPAN & KOREA

INTRODUCTION

"The blood of the martyrs is the seed of the church." So said Tertullian, one of the 2nd century Christian apologists. In many ways this applied to the first Christian believers in both Japan and Korea. The fruit of courageous mission work by 16th century Jesuit Christians resulted in there being approximately 300,000 believers in Japan by the early 1600s. Yet brutal persecution by the Japanese rulers sought to erase these Christian believers.

In many ways such persecution failed. When Japan opened up to foreign nations and allowed churches to be established in the mid-19th century, visiting missionaries found a diminutive yet faithful band of Christians. And while the overall percentage of Christians in Japanese society has remained small, they have made disproportionately great contributions to that society.

A similar narrative unfolded in Korea. Originally introduced to Korea from China, Christian faith took root. As in Japan, Korean rulers sought to crush the growing church. Thousands died for their faith in Christ. Christianity was banned until the 1870's. Eventually, however, especially after World War II and the Korean War, Christianity flourished. Today Megachurches, with evangelical and Pentecostal flavour, mark the nation. Thirty percent of the country claim to be Christian. Korean Christians are now intentionally taking the message of Jesus to the ends of the earth.

Though in different ways, Jesus has been a Game Changer in both of these far eastern nations.

WATCH EPISODE 11 'JAPAN & KOREA'

GETTING STARTED

What, if anything, surprises you from this episode about the story of Christianity in Japan and Korea?

REFLECTION

Read Acts 7:54-8:4. Reflect on the passages in light of the information you have learnt about Japan and Korea's beginnings with the Gospel.

DISCUSSION

1   *"The blood of the martyrs is the seed of the church."* Why does this apply to the two countries focussed on in this episode?

2   In light of this episode, read Luke 10:1-20. Take turns to share your response to one, or each of the following:

     (i)   A word or phrase that particularly captures your attention

     (ii) Where this passage intersects with your life at present

(iii) Any instruction, command, encouragement or challenge that this text brings to you at present.

3   Mark Noll comments about the arrival of Christianity in Japan in the 16th century: *"… the Christian message takes root when there is a strong presentation of the message and it meets a felt need in the population."* What do you think are some of the "felt needs" in your culture today?

4   The responses to the Gospel in Japan and Korea have been different. What might this tell us about how the mission of the Church needs to take cultural differences into account?

5   Christians were strongly persecuted by the rulers in Japan and in Korea during the early years. Why, do you think, is Christianity seen as suspicious and/or opposed by some countries, cultures and governments?

6 The early persecution of Christians in Japan often involved torturing one's family in an effort to get people to recant faith: *"… they would take your family and torture your family to try and get you to recant."* [Robert Woodberry] Read Matthew 10:32-39, Mark 3:31-34 and 7:10. How do you respond to the dilemma of loyalty to family *and* loyalty to Christ in our culture today? Do we "worship" family too much today?

7 Paul Yokota argues that the Christian Church in Japan *"tends to be inward looking, inside the church building."* To what extent could this critique be levelled at the Church in your country?

8 What strikes you about Billy Kim's personal story and journey to faith?

ACTION

Reflect on the use of the Fumi-e test, mentioned in the episode.

Try to imagine yourself in this scenario. As far as possible, reflect on what your response would have been to the choice to step on the picture, or not. What might be a rough equivalent in your cultural context, a situation where you are tested to deny or affirm your faith in Jesus? Look for an opportunity this week to graciously but boldly speak up about your faith.

"IF YOU ARE SAVED BY FAITH ALONE, COMPELLED FAITH IS NOT FAITH. ONLY TRUE FAITH SAVES YOU. SO, IF I FORCE YOU TO SAY OR DO SOMETHING, IT DOESN'T SAVE YOU, IT'S USELESS ... EVEN IF YOU'RE WRONG, YOU HAVE THE RIGHT TO BE WRONG. I HAVE TO CONVINCE YOU, BECAUSE ONLY TRUE FAITH WILL SAVE YOU."

ROBERT WOODBERRY

EPISODE 12
AMERICA

INTRODUCTION

Spanish conquistadors and adventurers had explored areas of the southern part of present-day America in the 16th century – South Carolina, Texas, Florida and even as far inland as the Grand Canyon. They founded Santa Fe in the north of New Mexico in 1609. Yet it was the colonies planted by the English in the north east of the continent that eventually laid the foundations for present day America. Commercial interests played a part in the formation of colonies from 1609 onwards. Most of those colonies were grounded in the faith of Jesus and a desire of the colonialists to follow and worship Him freely.

Today, the concept of "liberty" in the US is more usually interpreted in political and personal terms. The arrival in 1620 of the *Mayflower* brought Christians from England whose primary motivation was a yearning for *religious* liberty, not a craving for wealth. In doing so, they steeled the backbone of the thirteen colonies that first formed the "United States of America."

That sturdy, resounding drive for religious liberty played a significant role in moulding the American Constitution. Founding Fathers of the nation believed that faith was vital for freedom. Fuelled by such convictions, the United States became a seedbed for democracy, self-determination, generosity and Christian mission across the globe. Even though this did not create a perfect nation, Jesus was a Game Changer in shaping this new nation in the so-called New World. And the United States continues, for all of its faults, to be a significant force in taking the Good News of Jesus to the ends of the earth today.

WATCH EPISODE 12 'AMERICA'

GETTING STARTED

Read the following Bible passages dealing with the concept of freedom:

John 8:31-41; Acts 4:1-4, 18-20; Romans 6:15-23; Galatians 5:1-13; 1 Peter 2:16

REFLECTION

In your culture and setting, do you believe and feel as though you have genuine "freedom"? If so, in what aspects? How important to your everyday life is that feeling and actuality of liberty?

DISCUSSION

1   This episode strongly argues for the centrality of freedom, linked ultimately to the Bible and Christian faith, in the founding of the American state. Why do you think this is so important? Do you agree? Why or why not?

2 Consider Jesus' words about freedom in John 8:31-41. How, if at all, does Jesus' teaching here relate to the freedoms discussed in this episode?

3 Why is freedom of religion and worship so important for civil freedom in a nation?

4 Karl asks this question of Jay Milbrandt: *"Do you think that that sense of freedom of conscience and freedom of faith is still pervasive in America?"* Discuss this question in the context of your country and culture.

5 Christian missionaries are frequently maligned today but this episode argues the very opposite. Though very imperfect, missionaries do much good in our world. What have been some of the benefits? What have been some of the damaging aspects of Western mission work?

6 Os Guinness observes that Christians are a huge majority in America but have very little cultural impact. Why do you think that might be the case? What about the cultural impact of Christianity in your own situation?

7 Read 1 Corinthians 1:18-31 and 4:8-10. In light of these verses, how do you respond to the story of the missionary, John Chau in this episode? Was he an appropriate "fool for Christ" or just foolish?

ACTION

Make a list of the freedoms that are important to you. Spend some time considering what it would be like to live under a government that constrained or compelled your religious beliefs (or non-beliefs). Ponder what price you would pay to achieve that freedom.

NOTES

"THE CENTRE OF THE CHURCH IS CHANGING, SHIFTING TO THE SOUTHERN HEMISPHERE, AND I THINK OUR BROTHERS AND SISTERS IN THE WEST ARE STRUGGLING. THIS IS OUR TIME TO STAND UP AND TAKE THE GOSPEL FROM EVERYWHERE TO EVERYWHERE."

ERMIAS MAMO

EPISODE 13
20TH CENTURY MISSION

INTRODUCTION

In this episode, Lynn Cohick makes this observation: *"When you know that Jesus loves you and your sins are forgiven, you can't help but share it. And so, whether that means that you go to another country or you learn another language or you're just talking to your neighbour over the fence in the backyard, there's something compelling about the story that makes you want to share it."*

This comment goes to the heart of the best motivation for taking the message of Jesus to others, a central feature of the Christian faith: a desire to share "Good News". Followers of Jesus are to have a sense of mission to the world, compelled by love.

In recent years, that missionary impetus has been criticised heavily as being an aspect of Western colonialism and imperialistic expansion, especially in the late 18th through to the early 20th century. It is a criticism with some validity, yet across 2000 years of history the call of Jesus to share the Gospel with others has led hundreds of thousands of people to sacrificially go to the ends of the earth. They not only shared the message of Jesus. Hospitals were constructed. Schools were founded. The value of each individual was championed. Evils were challenged. In many parts of the world Jesus clearly was the Game Changer!

For around 1500 years, Christianity was predominantly a Western, European-based faith. Thus, from Europe and its colonies, missionaries spread out to the Global South and East. Usually this meant white people (often men) went to Asian, African and tribal peoples in the Americas, Australia and the Pacific.

The reality is radically different today. The Church in the West has weakened. The gravitational centre of Christian populations now thrums with energy south and east of the equator. Furthermore, the urbanisation of the world population has resulted in megacities blooming, into which pour people from every "nation, tribe, people and language" (Revelation 7:9). One result is that mission no longer flows from north to south and west to east. Missionaries from the South and East are coming to the West with the Good News of Jesus.

As this episode reveals, we may go to a different geographic location. We may speak to a different generation within our own culture, or we may share with a neighbour of a different cultural background, over our back fence or kitchen table. In all of these ways, if we follow Jesus, we can be missionaries to the ends of the earth. And we must be! Love demands it!

WATCH EPISODE 13 '20TH CENTURY MISSION'

GETTING STARTED

The Acts of the Apostles could be described as the first missionary history and textbook. Read these different stories of missionaries from that book: Acts 8:1-8; 26-35; 11:19-24; 12:25-13:4; 16:6-10.

REFLECTION

If you are a follower of Jesus, how does the title "missionary" sit with you when you apply it to yourself?

DISCUSSION

1   As you listened to this episode what

       (i)   surprised you?

       (ii) challenged you?

       (iii) encouraged you?

       (iv) motivated you?

2 How do you respond to this comment by Ermias Mamo at the opening segment of the episode: *"The centre of the Church is changing, shifting to the Southern Hemisphere, and I think our brothers and sisters in the West are struggling. This is our time to stand up and take the Gospel from everywhere to everywhere"?*

3 In your group, re-read and compare the following texts: Acts 8:1-8; 26-35; 11:19-24; 12:25-13:4; 16:6-10. They all describe mission work, but what do the texts tell you about that work?

4 Since 1910 to now, what have been the major shifts in world Christianity and its mission work?

5 The era of Western colonialism coincided with the *"Great Century of Missions"* [Ed Stetzer]. What were the blessings and what were the curses of that coincidence?

6 Look at Acts 15:1-22. How does this passage speak into the question of de-linking the Gospel from a particular culture so that different cultures can embrace Christian faith *"in many different forms"* [Dana Robert] and *"in a language that they understand best"* [Tefera Endalew].

7 Discuss this observation by Karl in the episode: *"You know, in the past, missionaries used to get onto boats and planes to go to the ends of the earth. But now the ends of the earth have come to our large cities. Going to the ends of the earth may mean simply crossing the street."* What are the implications of this for local churches? For you?

8 Eddie Arthur cautions us in the following terms about condemning the Church's link to western colonialism: *"Yeah, there were times when missionaries worked too closely to the colonial authorities. You can't deny that. But you can't typify a two-thousand-year-old movement just on that one thing."* What other issues in Church or mission history might it be helpful to take a long view rather than make a judgment on one point in time?

9 This final episode finishes with many of the series' guests reflecting on their understanding of where the "ends of the earth" are today. Which comments resonate with you and why? How can you apply that into your context?

ACTION

Make a list of people, with whom you have some form of reasonably regular contact, who are "from the ends of the earth" in some of the senses discussed at the end of this episode (different culture/language/generation/belief system). Think about how you can engage with them in sharing the Good News of Jesus in word and deed.

Make a deliberate effort at engagement this week. It might be as simple as asking them about their culture, having a meal with them, serving them in some way, asking for help from them or offering help to them. Pray for opportunities to share about Christ as you do this.

NOTES

NOTES

Jesus the Game Changer
DVD

Karl Faase

Jesus Christ has made an indelible mark on human history and he continues to do so through his followers. Many people today do not realise that the values western democracies are built on actually originate in the life and teaching of Jesus. In this series, host Karl Faase travels to the UK, USA, India, Singapore and Australia interviewing over thirty authors, academics and modern-day game changers about how the life and teaching of Jesus changed the world and why it matters.

Contributors include Rico Tice, John Ortberg, Paula Gooder, Eric Metaxas, and Christine Caine. The twin DVD pack contains ten 28 minutes episodes.

506-0-42495-575-6

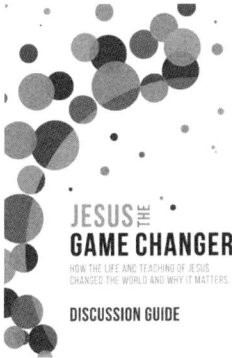

Jesus the Game Changer
Discussion Guide

Karl Faase

The discussion guide allows participants who watch *Jesus the Game Changer* to discuss the content and explore the influence of Jesus in the world. It provides an environment for open, reflective and honest questions emerging from the subjects of each DVD episode.

This guide is designed to help small groups navigate the material in *Jesus the Game Changer* in a manner that will help stimulate discussion and bring the issues into real life situations. Participants will be given the opportunity to consider how the key ideas presented in the series might impact their lives.

978-1-78078-181-5

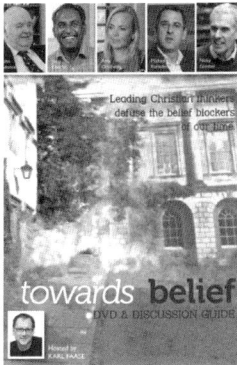

Towards Belief
DVD

Karl Faase

Is it reasonable to be a person of faith? How can we deal with issues of suffering, science, violence, abuse and the supernatural in our consideration of God? *Towards Belief* is a ten part DVD series that sets out to defuse the belief blockers of our time and is an essential resource for all churches and ministry groups committed to helping people explore Christian faith.

Contributors include John Lennox, Nicky Gumbel , Amy Orr-Ewing and John Dickson. The *Towards Belief* Set comes complete with two DVDs and a Discussion Guide for personal or group study.

978-0-98062-668-1

Authentic

We trust you enjoyed reading this book from Authentic. If you want to be informed of any new titles from this author and other releases you can sign up to the Authentic newsletter by scanning below:

Online:
authenticmedia.co.uk

Follow us: